FACT FINDERS

Educational adviser: Arthur Razzell

Pirates

Silas Martin

Illustrated by Eddie Brockwell, Jeff Burn, Dick Eastland,
Richard Hook, Roger Phillips and Temple Art
Designed by Faulkner/Marks Partnership

Macmillan Education Limited

© Macdonald Educational 1980

Adapted and published in
the United States by
Silver Burdett Company,
Morristown, N.J.
1980 Printing

ISBN 0-382-06465-8

Library of Congress
Catalog Card No. 80-50433

Pirates

Pirates on the Seas	page 4
Pirates of Long Ago	page 6
The Slave Raiders	page 9
The Spanish Main	page 10
Pirate Ships and Weapons	page 12
Pirates around the World	page 14
Women Pirates	page 16
Two Famous Pirates	page 18
The Last Pirates	page 20
Glossary	page 22
Index	page 23

Pirates on the Seas

In olden times, many of the ships that sailed the seas were pirate ships. Pirates were sea robbers. They used to attack other ships and rob them. They sometimes killed people as they were doing this.

You can see an English pirate ship attacking a Dutch vessel on the right. Today, there are very few pirates left.

Dutch ship 1650

English ship 1650

Pirates of Long Ago

There have been pirates on the seas for at least two thousand years.

Julius Caesar (above) was a great Roman leader. When he was young, he was captured by pirates in the Mediterranean Sea. His friends had to send money to free him. Later Caesar sailed back and captured the pirates. He had them put to death.

Viking longship

Viking raiders

The Viking people came from Scandinavia. Many of them set out in boats to attack Britain and other countries. They were early pirates. They killed and stole from many people in their raids.

Pirates often fought fierce battles like this one (left). The Spanish and English are fighting on board the ships.

The Slave Raiders

9

Many of the pirates in the Mediterranean Sea came from the Barbary coast of North Africa.

Most of these pirates were Moslems. They captured or killed thousands of Christians. The prisoners were taken back to cities in Africa. Here they were sold as slaves (below).

Christian prisoners

Moslem pirates

The Spanish Main

Spanish treasure ships carried gold from the Spanish Main (see map) to Spain. They were often attacked and robbed by pirates.

Henry Morgan (right) was an English pirate. Once his ships were trapped by the Spanish fleet. He escaped by sending fireships to burn and sink the Spanish boats. The English made him a hero.

Henry Morgan

Fireships

Pirate Ships and Weapons

Pirates liked to sail in ships that were fast and easy to handle. Many pirate ships were smaller than the ships they attacked. They could be manoeuvred more quickly than the big ships.

The Vikings used boats like the one below. Later pirates used ships like the one on the opposite page. They often took over and used any ships that they captured.

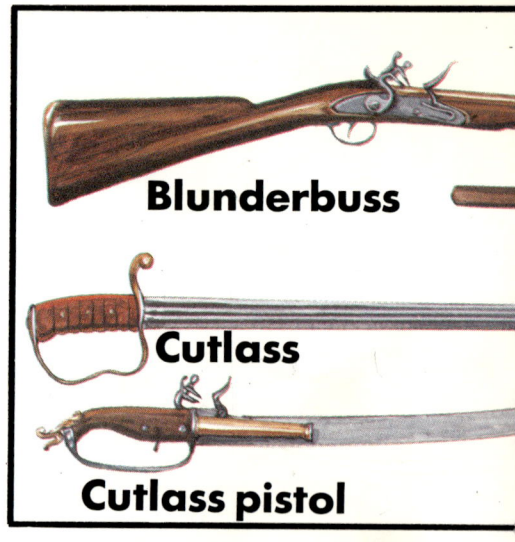

Blunderbuss

Cutlass

Cutlass pistol

Viking longship

Folding bayonet

Rigging hatchet

Dagger

Pirate ships were always very well armed. Only naval ships had a good chance of sinking them. When pirates boarded a ship, they used weapons like the ones on the left.

Pirate ships flew frightening flags. Most of them flew a skull and crossbones flag. Others flew a blood red 'Jolly Roger.' Nobody knows how the 'Jolly Roger' got its name.

Captured merchant ship

14 Pirates around the World

Bonnet

North Atlantic

Roberts

Spanish Main

South Atlantic

Honest sailors must have thought that there were pirates everywhere! The most dangerous places were the Spanish Main and the coasts of Africa.

Some pirates buried their treasure. They hoped to come back for it later. But many of them were caught and hung. Today some people hunt for the lost treasure.

Bart

These pictures show five famous pirates. The arrows point to the places where they most often attacked ships.

Dampier

Asia

Africa

Indian Ocean

Pacific Ocean

Avery

Australia

Women Pirates

The two most famous women pirates were Anne Bonny and Mary Read.
  Mary was very adventurous. She dressed as a man to become a sailor. Then she was captured by pirates and forced to join them.
Anne was a pirate on the same ship.

Mary Read

Anne believed Mary was a man. She fell in love with her. Mary had to tell Anne who she really was.

Later Mary married a sailor who the pirates had captured. She saved him by fighting his enemy for him. In the end Mary was captured.

Anne Bonny

Two Famous Pirates

Blackbeard's real name was Edward Teach. He used to twist lighted tapers in his hair. In the end he was captured and his head was chopped off.

Captain Kidd was sent to capture pirates in the Indian Ocean. Instead he became a pirate and was hanged (left). Many people do not believe that he became a pirate at all.

Captain Kidd

Blackbeard

The Last Pirates

By about 1840, there were only a few pirates left. Most of them were Chinese pirates. They attacked ships in the seas around China and Hong Kong.

The Chinese pirates sailed in boats called junks. You can see some pirate junks attacking a steamship below.

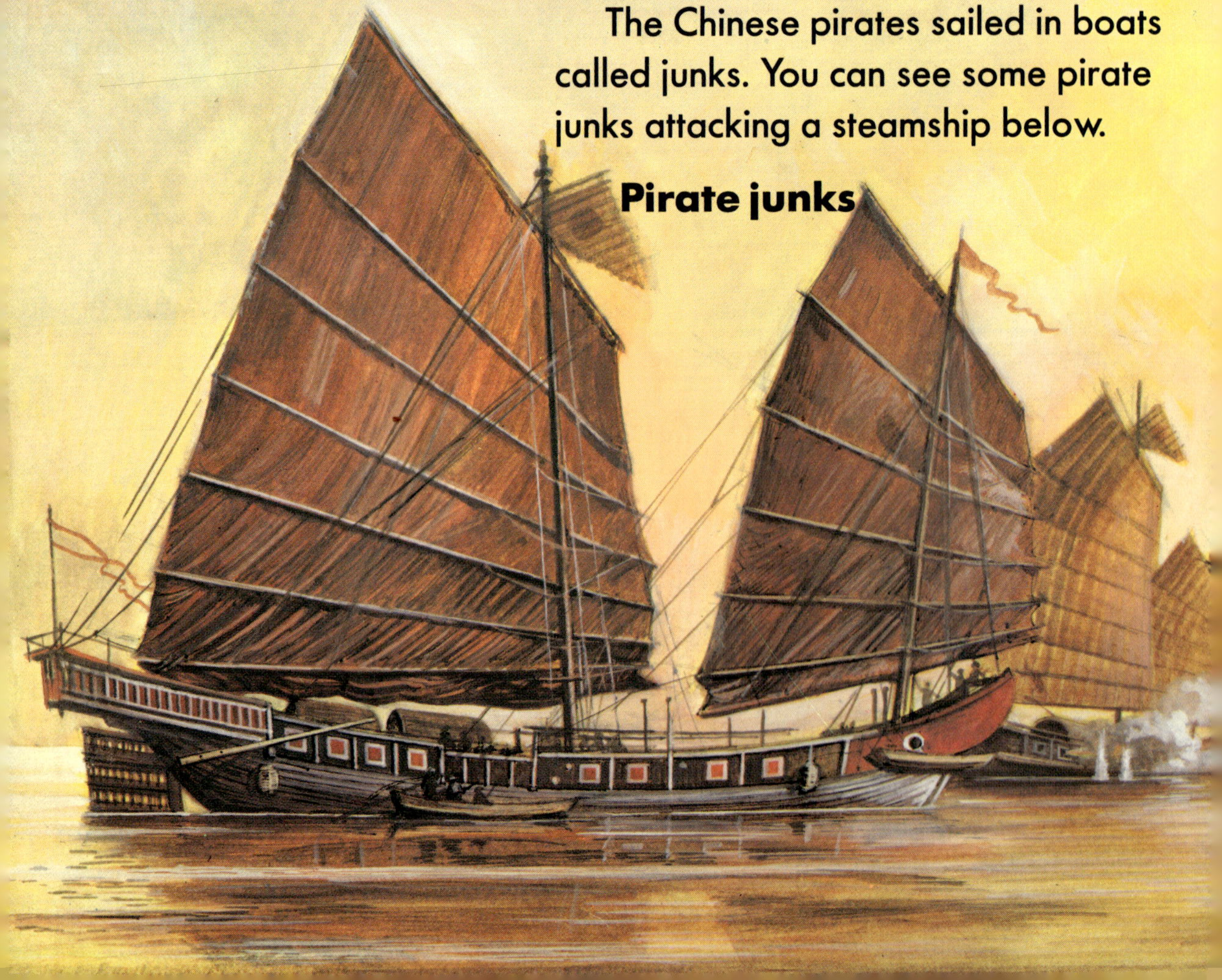

Pirate junks

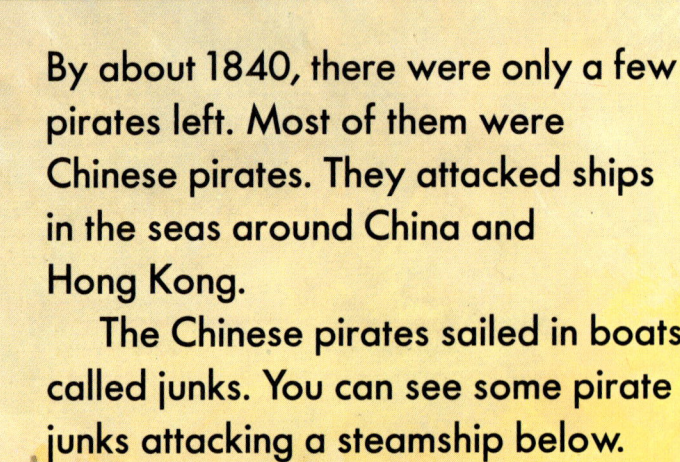

One of the last Chinese pirates was a woman called Madame Chung.

Many Chinese pirates became very rich. They stole cargoes from the ships they attacked. The British Navy helped to fight them. Now our seas are almost free of pirates.

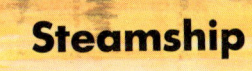

Steamship

Glossary

Barbary The old name for the coast of North Africa. The Barbary pirates sailed from the ports of Algiers, Tunis and Tripoli.

Blunderbuss A short old-fashioned gun. Blunderbusses fired several bullets all at once. They were very dangerous.

Fireships Ships that are filled with explosives and steered towards enemy ships. As the fireships hit the enemy ships, they explode into flames.

Junks Flat-bottomed sailing boats used in the Chinese seas.

Longships The long, narrow ships used by the Vikings. They had one large square sail and a large oar at the back which was used for steering. Each ship had a set of oars which was used in calm weather.

Moslems People who believe in and follow the ideas of the Prophet Mohammed. He taught that there is one god only. His message is written in a book called the Koran.

Spanish Main The old name for the sea between the West Indies and the South American mainland. It is now called the Caribbean Sea.

Vikings The people who lived in Scandinavia about a thousand years ago. Many Vikings left their homeland to raid neighbouring countries. Some eventually settled abroad and became peaceful traders.

Index

Africa 9, 14
Avery 15
Barbary coast 9, 22
Bart 15
Blackbeard 18
Blunderbuss 12, 22
Bonnet 14
Bonny, Anne 16-17
British Navy 21
Caesar, Julius 6
Captain Kidd 18
Chinese pirates 20-21
Christians 9
Dampier 15
Early pirates 6-7
Famous pirates 18-19
Fireships 10, 22
Flags 13
Indian Ocean 18
Jolly Roger 13
Julius Caesar 6
Junks 20, 22
Kidd, Captain 18
Madame Chung 21
Mediterranean Sea 6
Morgan, Henry 10
Moslems 9, 22
North Africa 9
Pirate ships 12
Pirate weapons 13
Prisoners 9
Read, Mary 16-17
Roberts 14
Roman pirates 6
Scandinavia 7, 22
Sea robbers 4
Skull and crossbones 13
Slave raiders 8-9
Spain 10
Spanish Main 10, 14, 22
Teach, Edward 18
Treasure 4, 14
Treasure ships 10
Viking longships 12, 22
Vikings 7, 12, 22
Women pirates 16-17, 21

Photo credits: The British Museum; Michael Holford; The National Maritime Museum; Werner Forman Archive

1 2 3 4 5 6 7 8 9 10— R —85 84 83 82 81 80